WORSHIP THAT TOUCHES HEAVEN

Micah Stampley

Published by World of Wonder Publishing

ISBN: 978-1-7350607-4-3- Print

ISBN: 978-1-7350607-5-0- Digital

Unless otherwise indicated, Scripture quotations are taken from [insert Bible translation used, e.g., *The Holy Bible, New International Version®*]. Used by permission. All rights reserved worldwide.

This book is a work of Christian inspiration and is intended to encourage, uplift, and challenge readers in their faith journey. It is not intended to substitute for pastoral counseling, theological training, or professional advice.

For more information and booking, please visit: micahstampley.org

Printed in the United States of America

CONTENTS

FOREWORD

_____

W hen people hear the name *Micah Stampley*, many think of the songs, the albums, the powerful moments of worship on stages around the world. But when I hear his name, I simply think of my husband—the man I've walked beside through joys, trials, victories, and valleys. And what I know to be true is this: Micah is a worshipper in every sense of the word, long before he is a worship leader.

I've watched him worship when no one was looking—at home in the quiet, in prayer with our children, or while facing seasons that would have caused many to give up. His love for God has always been steady, and his surrender has always been real. Worship is not something he does; it's who he is.

That's what makes this book so special to me. These words aren't just lessons or ideas on paper—they're the very things Micah has lived. His songs have reached nations, but his heart has always reached for God first. And in these pages, he invites you into that same pursuit: a life where worship is not a performance but a posture, not just a song but a way of living.

As you read, I hope you hear not only his voice as a minister, but also his heart as a man who loves God deeply. My prayer is that his journey inspires you to lean in closer, to make space for God's presence, and to discover worship as more than music—it's intimacy, it's surrender, it's life.

From my heart to yours, I can honestly say this book carries the fragrance of the life Micah lives every day. And I believe, as you turn these pages, you will encounter the same God who has carried and sustained us through every season.

With love,

Heidi

DEDICATION

This book is dedicated to my Lord and Savior, Jesus Christ—the Giver of life and the Creator of all things. Without Him, there is no me!

ACKNOWLEDGEMENTS

WORSHIP THAT TOUCHES HEAVEN

Deep thanks to the love of my life, Heidi Stampley, my greatest supporter and encourager, you inspire me to dream, I love you forever. To my children: Brandon, Micah, Adam, David, and Ariana, may the lessons in this book be a part of the spiritual legacy I leave for you, thank you for your love and support, . To my precious grandchildren—Olivia, Naomi, and Adah—you bring me joy beyond measure. To my heavenly angel, Mary, one day we will worship around the throne together.

To my amazing church family, Shift Global Ministries: you push me to grow every single day!

To my parents, Pastor Richard Stampley Sr., Pastor Delmarie Stampley, Pastor Ronald Jones Sr., and Missionary Walita Jones—I love and appreciate you all deeply.

To my spiritual covering, Dr. Bill Winston, and to all my mentors, mentees, friends, and loved ones: you are invaluable treasures in my life.

INTRODUCTION

_____

WORSHIP THAT TOUCHES HEAVEN

There are moments in Scripture that serve as mirrors—reflecting not only the actions of ancient Israel but also the tendencies of God's people today. One such moment is found in *1 Samuel 4,* a chapter heavy with lessons about faith, reverence, and the presence of God.

In this pivotal story, the Israelites marched into battle against the Philistines carrying the Ark of the Covenant, convinced that the presence of this sacred object alone would secure their victory. Yet, to their shock, they faced devastating defeat. How could this be? Wasn't the Ark the very symbol of God's glory and power?

This book is built on the foundation of that passage. It does not attempt to retell the story in full but instead uncovers principles, warnings, and revelations hidden within it—truths that still echo into our generation. The Israelites' mistake was not in desiring God's glory, but in mishandling it.

Here you will find both *cautionary reminders* of what happens when the glory is approached the wrong way and *prophetic encouragements* of how God intends His presence to transform lives, churches, and nations. Think of this as an invitation to walk into the text with fresh eyes—not to observe from the sidelines, but to enter into the lessons for yourself.

The battle of 1 Samuel 4 is not just their story. It is ours. And it is through their missteps that God shows us a better way forward.

WORSHIP THAT TOUCHES HEAVEN

By: Micah Stampley

CHAPTER 1:
WORSHIP ISN'T A PLAYLIST

L et's get this out of the way: worship is not a genre on your favorite streaming app. If it was, some of us would be spiritual Olympians by now—medalists in hand-lifting, tambourine- slapping, or perfectly harmonized shouts of "Yes, Lord!" But as comforting as our favorite worship artists is on repeat, true worship isn't a melody. It's not something you schedule between announcements and the sermon. Worship is intimacy—unfiltered, undignified, holy intimacy with our Heavenly Father.

In the Greek, the word for worship is *proskuneō*, which means "to kiss, like a dog licking his master's hand," or more reverently, "to bow down, to prostrate oneself in reverence and submission." (Yes, it starts a little awkward, but stay with me.) It describes closeness, humility, and honor. Worship isn't about mood lighting, smoke machines, or hitting the high note—it's about bringing our whole selves to the feet of a Holy God.

The Hebrew word *shachah* carries similar weight. It means "to bow down, to depress, to fall prostrate," showing that worship has always involved a physical and spiritual lowering of self to honor God. It's a posture more than a performance.

I once heard someone paraphrase it this way: "Worship is what you do when you finally realize you're not God."

That realization doesn't come from the right song list or slick production. It comes from deep, sacred intimacy—a relationship where vulnerability meets reverence. That kind of intimacy doesn't leave you the same. It always brings the glory. And by glory, I mean the tangible, weighty, all-consuming, knee-buckling manifested presence of God.

Before you get nervous, let me clarify: we don't chase goosebumps or try to manufacture the mystical. We pursue the face of God, and His glory responds. Just like fire follows sacrifice, glory follows intimacy. But intimacy requires something most modern Christians find inconvenient: surrender.

That brings me to a hard truth, straight from my sermon *Here Comes the Glory*. The Israelites in 1 Samuel 4 made a tragic mistake. Instead of seeking the face of God before battle, they decided to flex with the Ark of the Covenant like it was a holy good luck charm. They paraded His presence without consulting His heart. And it cost them dearly.

The Ark represented the glory of God—the weight of His presence. Mishandling it wasn't just a bad strategy; it was spiritual negligence. You can't bypass intimacy and expect victory. You can't manufacture presence without relationship.

As I said in that sermon: "Death shows up when there's no glory."

The absence of God's presence isn't neutral; it's dangerous. When leaders, churches, and individuals attempt to substitute real worship with emotional hype or polished programs, we risk becoming a shell of our former glory. Worse yet, we invite spiritual vulnerability. The enemy isn't scared of our sound system. He fears the glory.

You see, the Philistines knew something Israel forgot: as long as the glory remained, Israel was untouchable. But once the glory departed, so did their advantage.

Let's pause for a heart check.

- Are we worshipping to impress people or to encounter God?

- Are we offering polished performances or sacrificial surrender?

There's a vast difference between *singing about God* and *singing to Him.* True worship creates a throne. Psalm 22:3 reminds us, "God inhabits the praises of His people." That means He doesn't just pass through worship; He takes up residence in it.

You don't have to be a singer or musician to be a worshipper. But you do have to be a lover of God's presence. You do have to bring Him your heart, not just your habit. Worship isn't a vibe. It's a vehicle for glory.

And friend, here comes the glory.

CHAPTER 2:
GLORY IS THE EVIDENCE OF INTIMACY

You can always tell who's been with God. No, they don't walk around glowing like Moses (although that would be great for branding), but something about their atmosphere is different. Their words carry weight. Their presence carries peace. Their joy isn't performative—it's anchored.

You know why? Because glory follows intimacy.

Think of glory as the fragrance left behind after deep connection. When you've been in the arms of God, something stays on you. Like the scent of anointing oil on a priest's robe, the evidence lingers.

In Exodus 33:18, Moses didn't ask for a miracle or a microphone. He said, "Please, show me Your glory." That's what intimacy looks like—not asking God to show off, but asking Him to show up.

Glory doesn't descend for casual company. It visits covenant. Glory is the weight of God settling on lives that have made room for Him. The Hebrew word for glory is *kabod*, which means "weight" or "heaviness." It's not meant to crush us, but to remind us: this isn't a game. This is the holy presence of the Creator of the Universe.

One author paraphrased it this way: "Worship is when our hearts whisper 'yes' to the gravity of God's greatness."

Unfortunately, many churches have become experts at creating moments but strangers to true manifestations. We plan services with military precision and spiritual amnesia—forgetting the One we claim to be gathered for.

Let me say something bold: the enemy doesn't mind us having church. He minds us having glory.

When worship is intimate, it becomes disruptive—to fear, to depression, to religiosity, to sickness, to every plan of the enemy. Glory doesn't accommodate darkness; it evicts it. That's why Satan isn't intimidated by well-dressed congregations or eloquent sermons. But he trembles at the sound of true worship.

I've said it before, and I'll say it again: pastors, don't become co-conspirators with the enemy by stifling the flow of God's presence in your gatherings. Don't trade glory for growth strategies.

Don't replace anointing with analytics.

The world doesn't need more churches that look like coffee shops with TED Talks. The world needs places where people can encounter the power and presence of the Living God. Where the weight of His glory makes addictions break, tears flow, healing takes place, and people walk out whole.

Where there is glory, there is life. As Jesus said in John 10:10, "The thief comes only to steal and kill and destroy. I came that they may have life and have it more abundantly."

Worship is our entry point. Not hype. Not gimmicks. Worship.

Real, raw, vulnerable, holy, tear-stained, knee-bent worship. Not to get something from God, but to give everything to Him. That's what brings the glory.

And I hear it again...

Here comes the glory.

CHAPTER 3:
MISHANDLING THE ARK: WHEN WORSHIP LOSES REVERENCE

WORSHIP THAT TOUCHES HEAVEN

There's a dangerous thing happening in many churches today—worship has lost its reverence. The Ark of the Covenant, the symbol of God's manifest glory in the Old Testament, was never something to be handled lightly. But when worship becomes casual, prideful, or entertainment- driven, we risk doing exactly what Israel did in 1 Samuel 4–7: carrying the presence of God without the weight of His glory.

In 1 Samuel 4, the Israelites went to battle against the Philistines and were losing. So they brought out the Ark of the Covenant, assuming that God's presence would guarantee them victory. But they didn't ask for God's direction. They didn't inquire of the Lord. They didn't consecrate themselves. They presumed. And they were defeated.

The glory didn't protect them—because reverence was missing.

We often read this text and think, "How could they be so foolish?" But many of us today are doing the same thing. We sing, we shout, we dance, we have the Ark (symbolically), but we've lost the fear of the Lord. We treat worship like a job, the platform like a stage, and God's presence like a special effect.

Here's the reality:

You can be gifted and still dangerous if you're not reverent.

Yes, you read that right. Gifts without reverence are hazardous.

David was gifted. Uzzah was probably sincere. The sons of Eli were ordained. Saul was anointed. But when reverence was absent— *so was God's favor.*

Worship, in its truest form, is never about our talent—it's about our **tremble**. We must carry the weight of His glory with holy awe, not just harmonic skill. When the presence becomes common, it becomes mishandled. The Ark is still holy.

Let's pause here. Let this sink in:

You can sing the house down and still miss heaven.

You can command a crowd but not carry the cloud.

You can prophesy, play, and preach—and still provoke judgment—if you treat God's presence like a prop.

When David tried to return the Ark to Jerusalem in 2 Samuel 6, he did it the wrong way at first— placing it on a cart, likely influenced by how the Philistines handled it in 1 Samuel 6. When Uzzah reached out to steady the Ark, he was struck down. Why? Because even with the right intentions, they carried the glory the wrong way.

David was devastated. But after studying the law and sanctifying the Levites, he learned the lesson: **God's glory must be carried on the shoulders of consecrated men—not on carts of convenience.**

This is where many of us have erred. We've placed the glory on carts of:

- Production instead of purity
- Popularity instead of presence
- Charisma instead of character
- Ambition instead of anointing

We don't need better platforms—we need better priests.

It's worth noting that Uzzah's name means "strength." This implies that Uzzah reached out in his own human strength to steady what only *divine reverence* could handle. We cannot protect the presence of God through fleshly effort. We must instead posture ourselves in humility, obedience, and holiness.

Even our most sincere intentions can't make up for disobedience. This chapter is not an indictment. It's a **call to alignment**.

The Church must recover the fear of the Lord in worship. Not fear in a tormenting sense, but *yir'ah* (Hebrew: the awe-filled, trembling respect that causes a person to bow low and walk upright.

When we lose reverence, we lose access. When we handle the holy casually, we handle it criminally.

Let's not just worship in spirit. Let's worship in **spirit and truth** (John 4:24).

Let's not just chase moments—let's host the **Majesty**. Let's not mishandle the Ark.

God's glory is not a gig. It's not a vibe. It's not a genre. It's sacred.

So yes—**you can be gifted and still dangerous if you're not reverent.**

But the beautiful news is: when we restore the reverence, we prepare the room for glory to return.

And that changes *everything*.

CHAPTER 4:
WHEN GLORY
GOES MISSING

WORSHIP THAT TOUCHES HEAVEN

"Ichabod"—the glory has departed.

—1 Samuel 4:21 (NIV)

L et's be real—most people don't even realize when the glory is missing. The lights are still on. The sound is excellent. The band is tight. The setlist is trendy. But heaven? Silent. God's presence? Uninvited.

Welcome to the age of impressive worship *without* intimacy.

Let's revisit a powerful moment from Scripture: **1 Samuel 4**. Israel went to battle assuming that having the Ark—the symbol of God's presence—was enough. They didn't consult God, didn't seek His direction. They just said, "Let's bring the Ark. Surely, that will guarantee victory!" In other words: "Let's bring the *appearance* of glory and hope God endorses it."

They *mishandled the presence of God*—treated it like a good-luck charm. And what happened? The Ark was captured. Eli's sons died. And when the news reached Eli, he fell back in shock and died. His daughter-in-law, in her final moments before death, gave birth and named the child "**Ichabod**," meaning **"the glory has departed."** *(Hebrew: 'î-kābōd')*

What a tragic moment. But it raises a deep, painful question we must ask ourselves: **Could we be operating in ministry while God's glory has already left the building?**

Worship Without God?

It's a frightening reality—performing for an audience of people while no longer hosting the presence of God. In the Greek, the word *doxa* means **glory**, but it goes deeper than just brightness or light. It implies **weight, honor, and divine radiance**. In worship, *doxa* must rest on us, not just pass through the room. If it's not transforming us, it's only visiting.

The challenge in this generation is that many know how to *sing* about Him but don't know how to *commune* with Him. We've learned the keys and chords of worship but abandoned the *posture* of worship.

Let's pause and ask ourselves honestly:

Are we producing sounds that echo heaven, or simply noise that entertains earth?

When Talent Outpaces Surrender

One of the most dangerous things in worship ministry is when our **gift** takes us places that our

character and **intimacy** cannot sustain us.

Let's face it—God's presence is not impressed by our range, runs, riffs, or rhythm. What moves Him is **surrender**. Psalm 24:3-4 (NIV) says:

"Who may ascend the mountain of the Lord? Who may stand in his holy place? The one who has clean hands and a pure heart…"

Worship is not about "ascending the stage," it's about ascending **the hill of the Lord**. It's not about the highest note, but the **highest honor**—to dwell where He is.

A.W. Tozer once said (and we're paraphrasing here):

"The church that cannot recognize when the Spirit has departed will soon settle for the imitation."

In other words, you can manufacture moments, but you can't manufacture **glory**.

Protecting the Presence

The Ark of the Covenant represented the **manifested presence of God**. The mistake Israel made was assuming that God's favor would automatically follow their actions. But God doesn't follow *formulas*—He responds to **fellowship**.

When David later brought the Ark back to Jerusalem (2 Samuel 6), he did it *right*. He worshipped with abandon. He consulted God. He sacrificed along the way. He honored the weight and *worth* of God's presence. He danced so radically that it made the religious folks uncomfortable. That's what worship that protects the glory looks like—*reverent, joyful, sacrificial, and free.*

Let that be our standard again.

Worship Leaders, It Starts With Us

To every worship leader, musician, and pastor reading this: **The glory of God is not our background music—it's our lifeline.**

If we're too tired to seek Him, too distracted to wait on Him, or too proud to admit we've missed Him… then we are preparing a place for *Ichabod*, not *Emmanuel*.

God's not looking for the perfect voice. He's looking for the prepared heart. He's not searching for performers. He's searching for **priests**.

In Hebrew, the word for *glory* is **kābōd**, meaning **"weight" or "honor."** When we mishandle the weight, we risk losing the wonder. The weight of His glory cannot be carried by entertainment or ego—it must rest on **intimacy and obedience**.

Closing Thoughts:

Let this chapter be a call to remembrance and repentance. It's time to ask:

Is the glory still here? And if not, what must I change to bring it back?

In the next chapter, we will uncover what happens *after* the glory is restored—and how God intends for it to **remain**, not just visit.

Until then, search your heart. Ask God to reveal any "Ichabod" moments. And invite Him, again, to dwell in your worship.

CHAPTER 5:
THE SOUND MIND OF A WORSHIPPER

———————

A Worshipper who can sing but cannot think clearly is a spiritual contradiction. Worship, at its deepest level, doesn't bypass the mind; it renews it. This chapter is not about musical notes or vocal acrobatics—it's about what happens between your ears when your heart is bowed in worship. Because if the mind is confused, distracted, or tormented, the worship becomes contaminated.

Paul writes in **2 Timothy 1:7 (NIV)**: *"For the Spirit God gave us does not make us timid, but gives us power, love and self-discipline."* The word translated as **"self-discipline"** or **"sound mind"** in some versions is the Greek word **sōphronismos**, which refers to a mind that is disciplined, clear, and under divine restraint. It's not just about being sane—it's about being **spiritually sober, emotionally grounded**, and **mentally aligned** with God.

There is a kind of worship that makes noise, and another that makes impact. The difference often lies in the state of the Worshippers's mind. You can't release heaven's sound if your internal world is full of static.

Have you ever tried to tune into a radio station but the signal kept fading? That's what it's like trying to hear God with a cluttered mind. When your emotions are all over the place and your thoughts are racing, you can't discern the still, small voice of the Father. But worship—true, Spirit-led worship—brings alignment. It centers the soul. It grounds the heart. It recalibrates the mind. Worship creates an atmosphere where anxiety has to bow, and torment has to back off.

Let's be clear: having a sound mind doesn't mean you'll never struggle. It means that in your struggle, you have an anchor. In worship, God becomes your anchor. Your internal chaos meets

His eternal calm. That's why when David was being hunted like an animal, he still wrote songs of confidence. *"The Lord is my light and my salvation—whom shall I fear? The Lord is the stronghold of my life—of whom shall I be afraid?"* (Psalm 27:1). That's not denial. That's a sound mind under divine influence.

Some of us are so used to singing about peace that we never stop long enough to let God give it to us. But real worship makes room for healing in the mind. It makes space for deliverance in the thought life. Some worshippers need more than a new song; they need **inner healing**. Anxiety, depression, intrusive thoughts—all of it must come subject to the atmosphere created by surrendered worship.

Jesus was the perfect worshipper, not because He sang better than anyone, but because He walked in perfect submission to the Father. In **John 5:19**, Jesus said, *"Very truly I tell you, the Son can do nothing by himself; he can do only what he sees his Father doing."* This isn't limitation. This is power under control.

Submission is not weakness. It is the access point of strength. **Obedience does not dilute the anointing—it deepens it.** The Greek word for obedience, **hupakoē**, means "to listen under." In worship, we come under the voice of the Father. We don't sing to impress Him; we sing to align with Him. A sound mind is not just a calm mind; it is a mind tuned in to the frequency of heaven.

Some of the greatest breakthroughs in worship happen **not** when the music is loud but when the soul is quiet. When the worship leader is no longer performing and the room is no longer spectating, something holy happens. The glory enters. The soul breathes. The mind settles. And the Father speaks.

This is what the glory does. It doesn't just fill rooms. It fills minds. It flushes out fear. It disinfects toxic thinking. It reminds you who you are and whose you are. Worship, in its purest form, is a spiritual detox.

Let this be the cry of the worshippers in this hour: "Lord, heal my mind so I can host Your glory." Because you can't carry what you haven't made room for. And a chaotic mind has no room for glory.

So take inventory of your thoughts. Confront what doesn't belong. Get therapy if needed. Get counsel. But above all—get into God's presence. Because in His presence is fullness of joy, clarity of thought, and peace that passes all understanding.

A sound mind isn't a luxury for the worshippers. It is a requirement. Without it, we build atmospheres that attract emotions, not encounters. But with it, we become holy conductors of God's presence.

Because in the end, the best worship isn't heard first. It's discerned. And you can't discern the voice of the Spirit with a mind full of noise.

So what's the practical takeaway? Worship doesn't just prepare your spirit for encounter—it recalibrates your mind for alignment. It takes the chaos of life and submits it to the order of heaven. It takes broken thought patterns and runs them through the filter of God's truth.

The Psalmist said it best: *"Why, my soul, are you downcast? Why so disturbed within me? Put your hope in God, for I will yet praise him, my Savior and my God"* (Psalm 42:11, NIV). Notice the discipline there—David speaks to his soul and commands it to hope and worship. That's a sound mind in action: not letting the inner storm dictate the song, but letting the song redirect the storm.

Let's not just be Worshipperss with lifted hands but scattered thoughts. Let's be whole Worshipperss

—spirit, soul, and mind, aligned before the Father. Because when the mind is anchored, the worship is unshakable. And when the worship is unshakable, the glory can rest.

CHAPTER 6:
THE COST OF CARRYING GLORY

WORSHIP THAT TOUCHES HEAVEN

G lory is heavy. That's not poetic—it's biblical. The Hebrew word for glory, **kabod**, literally means "weight." And that weight doesn't just rest anywhere; it looks for consecrated shoulders.

In the Old Testament, the Levites were chosen to carry the Ark of the Covenant—the physical symbol of God's glory. It wasn't strapped to oxen carts like luggage. It was carried by consecrated men who had prepared themselves to bear the weight of holiness. (See 1 Chronicles 15:14–15).

Here's the part we miss: glory is transferable, but it's not cheap. You can borrow someone else's song, but you can't borrow their sacrifice. You can imitate their sound, but you can't duplicate their oil. The oil only flows where there has been crushing.

Let's be honest—modern Christianity often wants glory without groaning, anointing without altar, fire without fuel. But here's the pattern we see all through Scripture: **every time God shows up in glory, someone has already laid something down in sacrifice.**

- Abraham laid Isaac on the altar, and the glory of God's provision was revealed (Genesis 22).

- Elijah laid the bull on Mount Carmel, and the fire of God fell (1 Kings 18).

- Jesus laid His life down, and the glory of resurrection broke through (John 17:1–5).

Glory costs.

The Apostle Paul said in Romans 12:1 (NIV): *"Therefore, I urge you, brothers and sisters, in view of God's mercy, to offer your bodies as a living sacrifice, holy and pleasing to God—this is your true and proper worship."* Notice—worship isn't the song you bring; it's the sacrifice you become.

The Cart of Convenience

Remember when David first tried to bring the Ark back to Jerusalem? He put it on a cart, just like the Philistines had done. But when Uzzah reached out to steady it, he dropped dead (2 Samuel 6). Why? Because even good intentions can't replace God's instructions.

Many of us are still guilty of placing the glory on carts of convenience—

- Programs instead of prayer
- Entertainment instead of intercession
- Skill instead of surrender

But carts don't carry glory—consecrated shoulders do. And consecrated shoulders belong to consecrated lives.

The Call to Levites Today

If you lead worship, preach, play, or serve on the altar, you're not just a performer—you're a priest. The modern Levite doesn't carry an Ark overlaid with gold; they carry the very presence of God in their lives. And God is still particular about who carries His glory.

Don't misunderstand me—this isn't about perfection. It's about posture. Holiness isn't flawlessness—it's "set apart-ness." A Levite's life says: *"I will not touch what defiles. I will not treat as common what is holy. I will carry the weight, even when it costs me."*

As one author once wrote: *"The anointing that costs you nothing will accomplish nothing."*

Closing Thought

The cost of glory is high, but so is the reward. When the Levites carried the Ark into the Jordan, the waters parted (Joshua 3:15–16). When David carried the Ark into Jerusalem with dancing and sacrifice, the whole nation rejoiced (2 Samuel 6:14–15).

Glory doesn't just rest where it is wanted—it rests where it is **weighted.** And if you're willing to pay the cost, you'll find that the weight of His glory is also the strength of your life.

CHAPTER 7:
WORSHIP AS WARFARE

WORSHIP THAT TOUCHES HEAVEN

Worship isn't just intimacy—it's artillery. Every time you open your mouth in true worship, hell loses ground. Every time you lift your hands in surrender, chains fall. Every time your song rises from a surrendered heart, the kingdom of darkness trembles.

That's why the enemy fights worship so hard—because he knows worship is a weapon.

The Jehoshaphat Strategy

One of my favorite examples is in 2 Chronicles 20. King Jehoshaphat faced a massive army he couldn't defeat. Instead of sharpening swords, he sharpened his worship. He appointed singers to go ahead of the army declaring: *"Give thanks to the Lord, for his love endures forever"* (v. 21).

And what happened? The Lord set ambushes against the enemy. Jehoshaphat didn't win with spears; he won with songs. Worship confused the opposition and shifted the outcome.

Worship in the Midnight Hour

Paul and Silas understood this too. Beaten, chained, and thrown into a Philippian jail, they didn't cry or complain. At midnight, they worshipped. And Scripture says: *"Suddenly there was such a violent earthquake that the foundations of the prison were shaken. At once all the prison doors flew open, and everyone's chains came loose"* (Acts 16:26, NIV).

Catch that: not just *their* chains, but *everyone's* chains came loose. Worship is so powerful that it doesn't just free you—it frees everyone connected to you. Your worship can break the atmosphere over your family, your church, your city.

Jericho Walls Still Fall

And who can forget Jericho? God instructed Israel not to attack, but to march and to shout. No weapons. No catapults. Just obedience and worship. And on the seventh day, when the trumpet sounded and the people shouted, the walls fell flat (Joshua 6:20).

Worship isn't passive—it's prophetic. It tears down walls, confuses the enemy, and builds a throne for God to reign.

Worship Silences the Enemy

Psalm 8:2 (NIV) says: *"Through the praise of children and infants you have established a stronghold against your enemies, to silence the foe and the avenger."* Even the weakest voice, when lifted in pure worship, is strong enough to silence hell itself.

Closing Thought

When you worship, you're not just singing—you're swinging. You're not just clapping—you're clashing with the kingdom of darkness. Worship invites God to fight on your behalf, and when He fights, He never loses.

So don't underestimate your song. Don't belittle your hallelujah. Don't silence your shout. The devil doesn't care if you preach well, but he shakes when you worship well.

Because worship is not just what touches heaven. It's what makes hell nervous.

CHAPTER 8:
HOSTING THE PRESENCE, NOT JUST VISITING IT

_____

(Difference between moments and abiding presence; revival as a lifestyle, not an event)

T here's a difference between having a guest visit your house and having someone live in your house. When a guest visits, you tidy up, prepare your best dishes, and create a temporary atmosphere of welcome. But when someone lives there, their presence shapes the rhythm of the home. Furniture may be rearranged, routines are adjusted, and every room carries evidence of their life.

The same principle applies to our relationship with God. Many believers know how to "visit" His presence — in a powerful worship service, a revival meeting, or a prayer gathering — but far fewer know how to **host His presence** daily. One is an event; the other is a lifestyle. One faces when the music stops; the other transforms every corner of your life.

The Ark as a Symbol of Hosting

In the Old Testament, the Ark of the Covenant represented God's tangible presence. Israel carried it into battle, and victory followed (Joshua 6:6–20). But the Ark wasn't meant to be a war accessory; it was meant to be **hosted**. Consider Obed-Edom in 2 Samuel 6:11: *"The ark of the*

Lord remained in the house of Obed-Edom the Gittite for three months, and the Lord blessed him and his entire household."

Obed-Edom didn't just experience a moment of God's presence. He lived in it. Hosting the Ark shifted the atmosphere of his home and released blessings over everything he owned. This is what happens when we go from **moments of revival** to **a culture of revival**.

From Goosebumps to Habitation

Too many of us chase after goosebumps in worship, thinking that emotional highs are the measure of God's nearness. But God never intended to give us visitation rights — He wants residency. Jesus said in John 14:23, *"Anyone who loves me will obey my teaching. My Father will love them, and we will come to them and make our home with them."*

Notice the word: *home.* God isn't looking for weekend accommodations. He's looking for people who will prepare a dwelling place, not just a guest room.

Revival Is Not an Event

Modern Christianity often treats revival like a scheduled event: flyers, guest speakers, and a set time frame. But true revival is not penciled onto a church calendar — it is **a lifestyle of God's abiding presence.**

Smith Wigglesworth once said, *"We are to be a people that are full of God, full of His presence, full of His glory."* Revival that burns only for a week is human fire; revival that continues for generations is hosted by people who make their entire lives a sanctuary.

Hosting the Presence Practically

How do we shift from visiting to hosting?

1. **Cultivate Daily Altars** – Just as Abraham, Isaac, and Jacob built altars wherever they went, we must create space daily where God is honored. This can be in prayer, worship, or intentional quietness before Him.

2. **Guard the Atmosphere of Your Home** – Ask: *What plays in my living room? What conversations fill the dinner table?* Hosting His presence means aligning every room with His Spirit.

3. **Value Obedience Over Feelings** – Emotions fluctuate, but His presence abides with those who walk in obedience (John 14:21). Hosting is less about how you feel and more about how you live.

4. **Prioritize Fellowship With Him** – Just as a housemate notices if they're ignored, the Holy Spirit desires ongoing interaction. Paul's closing words in 2 Corinthians 13:14 remind us: *"May the fellowship of the Holy Spirit be with you all."*

Illustration: The Lamp Versus the Match

Think of the difference between lighting a match and tending a lamp. A match burns brightly, but only for a moment. A lamp, when fueled with oil, burns steadily and lights the house continuously. Too many believers live like matches — striking in revival meetings but quickly burning out. God calls us to be lamps, filled with the oil of His Spirit, burning without ceasing (Matthew 25:1–13).

Living With Awareness

To host the presence means you carry Him into the grocery store, into board meetings, into traffic jams, into parenting moments. Revival is not just an altar call; it is **a way of being.**

Reflection Questions

1. Am I living as if God only "visits" me, or have I truly made Him at home in my life?

2. What practical changes can I make in my home to create an atmosphere that welcomes His presence?

3. Do I treat revival as a temporary event or as a lifestyle I am called to live daily?

Too many churches and Worshipperss settle for moments. A powerful song, a moving testimony, an altar call—it's all beautiful, but if glory only *visits*, it leaves when the lights go out. Hosting the presence of God means creating an environment, a lifestyle, where His glory can dwell continuously.

Jesus said in John 14:23 (NIV): *"Anyone who loves me will obey my teaching. My Father will love them, and we will come to them and make our home with them."* Notice: God isn't just stopping by. He's making a home. That's the heart of hosting the presence—inviting Him to settle, not just shine briefly.

The Difference Between Moments and Abiding Presence

A moment is fleeting. It might make you weep, feel lifted, or cry out in awe—but when the moment ends, you're back to life as usual. Abiding presence, however, transforms how you live. It touches your decisions, your family, your work, your relationships. It turns daily life into worship.

- **Moment:** "Wow, that worship set me on fire."
- **Abiding presence:** "I am fire because He dwells in me."

One practical way to host the presence is through daily surrender. Romans 12:1 (NIV) instructs us: *"Offer your bodies as a living sacrifice, holy and pleasing to God—this is your true and proper worship."* Not Sunday-only, not event-only. Continuous, intentional, holy living becomes the altar upon which His glory rests.

Revival isn't a Saturday night event. It's a lifestyle. The early church in Acts didn't schedule revival nights—they lived in the presence of the Spirit, prayed continuously, shared everything, and worshiped without reservation. The result? Transformation, miracles, and unshakable faith.

Practical Hosting

- Guard your heart. Intimacy with God begins inside.

- Protect your atmosphere. Avoid distractions that push out the glory.

- Invite Him continually. Prayer, praise, obedience, study of His Word—it's all a continual "open door" to God.

Hosting the presence is costly—but like the Levites, the weight of glory is not a burden; it's a blessing that transforms everything around you.

CHAPTER 9:
THE PROPHETIC
SOUND OF WORSHIP

———————

W orship doesn't just express faith—it declares the future. There's a sound that shifts nations, opens heaven, and releases God's plans into the earth. Prophetic worship speaks before it happens; it calls things that are not as though they were.

Habakkuk 2:14 (NIV) says: *"For the earth will be filled with the knowledge of the glory of the Lord, as the waters cover the sea."* Worship is one of the primary ways that "knowledge of glory" becomes manifest on the earth.

Worship as a Prophetic Voice

When Jehoshaphat appointed singers ahead of the army, they weren't just encouraging the soldiers—they were declaring the victory God had already promised. Their sound shifted the natural outcome. Worship speaks heaven's reality into the earth.

- **Prophetic declarations:** When worship aligns with God's heart, it doesn't merely express what we know; it announces what heaven intends.

- **Shifts nations:** Corporate worship, prayer, and praise have historically changed kingdoms. Remember Daniel in Babylon? Prayer and worship unlocked angelic intervention (Daniel 10).

- **Opens heaven:** Jesus said, *"Where two or three gather in my name, there am I with them"* (Matthew 18:20, NIV). Even the smallest gathering, lifted in true worship, can open the heavens.

The Sound That Commands

Hebrew and Greek insights remind us that sound is more than vibration. The word *qol* in Hebrew means voice, sound, or utterance—it carries authority. Worship uttered in Spirit and truth has the power to change circumstances.

- Prophetic worship calls breakthrough.

- Prophetic worship silences opposition.

- Prophetic worship shifts atmospheres.

When Paul and Silas worshipped at midnight, the chains fell. When Jehoshaphat's singers declared God's promises, the enemy destroyed themselves. Prophetic sound isn't about performance— it's about **alignment with God's voice**, and when worship aligns, heaven moves first.

CHAPTER 10:
WORSHIP THAT TOUCHES HEAVEN, CHANGES EARTH

WORSHIP THAT TOUCHES HEAVEN

H ere's the climax: worship that truly touches heaven doesn't just lift hearts—it transforms societies. It changes churches, communities, families, and cities.

Psalm 149:6–9 (NIV) says: *"Let the high praises of God be in their mouths and a double-edged sword in their hands, to inflict vengeance on the nations, to bind their kings with fetters, their nobles with shackles of iron, to carry out the sentence written against them."* Worship is both encounter and action. It's intimate devotion and earth-shaking authority.

The Multiplier Effect

True worship always expands:

- **Personal:** Our hearts and minds are aligned, fears are broken, joy and peace flow.

- **Family:** Worship opens homes to blessing and protection.

- **Church:** Worship leaders who carry the weight of God's presence ignite the congregation; revival spreads through obedience and intimacy.

- **Society:** Public worship and intercession bring light into darkness, turning cities and nations toward God.

A Call to Boldness

Too many believers treat worship as entertainment or a hobby. But when we step into the fullness of its purpose, worship becomes **the instrument God uses to restore, heal, and liberate the earth.**

We are called to be more than spectators of glory. We are carriers, conduits, and heralds. Your worship can touch heaven, and the echo can shake hell, heal families, and restore communities.

Final Thought

Friend, if we approach worship as a lifestyle, a prophetic declaration, and a force that shifts heaven and earth, we will see transformation that goes far beyond our imagination.

Worship is not just what we do—it is who we are. It is how we live, how we pray, and how we carry God's presence into every corner of life.

Here comes the glory. And it doesn't just visit. It stays. It moves. It changes everything it touches.

CHAPTER 9:
THE PROPHETIC SOUND OF WORSHIP

(How worship releases prophetic declarations, shifts nations, and opens heaven)

Worship has always been more than melody; it is a **weapon, a prophecy, and a decree** wrapped in sound. Heaven itself was birthed in song—when the morning stars sang together and all the angels shouted for joy (Job 38:7). The prophetic sound of worship is not confined to instruments or voices—it is heaven's voice amplified through surrendered vessels on earth. When released, it shakes nations, silences demons, and opens doors no human hand can pry open.

Prophetic worship declares the future into the present. It shifts atmospheres. It disrupts the enemy's strategies. It proclaims God's reign until the kingdoms of this world bow to the Kingdom of our Lord.

1. Worship That Wins the War: Jehoshaphat's Army

In 2 Chronicles 20, King Jehoshaphat faced an impossible coalition of enemies. Outnumbered and overwhelmed, he did something illogical—he placed **singers ahead of soldiers**. Instead of sharpening spears, he sharpened songs. Instead of lifting swords, they lifted the sound: *"Give thanks to the Lord, for His love endures forever."*

And heaven responded. Confusion broke out in the enemy's camp, and they destroyed one another. Israel didn't just win a battle—they plundered for three days.

This is prophetic worship: sound that speaks what God will do before it happens. Their song was not reactive—it was **proactive prophecy**. They didn't sing because they saw victory. They sang, and **victory appeared.**

2.　The Song of Deborah: A Prophetic Anthem for a Nation

In Judges 5, Deborah and Barak sang a victory song after Sisera's defeat. But notice—the song was more than celebration. It was **prophetic instruction** for generations.

- It named tribes that fought and tribes that stayed behind.

- It declared curses over indifference and blessings over bravery.

- It called out Jael's courage as a model for Israel's daughters.

Deborah's song shaped identity and culture. It was both **journalism and prophecy**—recording what God had done while declaring what He expected His people to embody moving forward.

Prophetic worship doesn't just fill the air with melodies. It tells a people **who they are** and **who God is calling them to be**.

3.　Hannah's Song: Prophecy in the Midst of Personal Pain

In 1 Samuel 2, after years of barrenness, Hannah sang: *"The Lord brings death and makes alive; he brings down to the grave and raises up. The Lord sends poverty and wealth; he humbles and he exalts."*

Her song was birthed in personal breakthrough, yet it **prophesied national destiny**. She declared a reversal anointing that would echo into Mary's Magnificat centuries later. Her worship became a prophetic chain reaction across generations.

Prophetic worship often flows from the womb of pain, releasing a sound that not only heals the singer but sets the course for nations.

4.　Paul and Silas: Midnight as a Prophetic Stage

In Acts 16, beaten and chained in a Philippian jail, Paul and Silas began singing hymns at midnight. This was not background music—it was warfare. Suddenly, a violent earthquake shook the foundations of the prison. Doors flew open. Chains fell off—not just theirs, but everyone's.

That is the power of prophetic sound. It **breaks collective bondage**. Worship that carries heaven's frequency does not just free the worshipper; it liberates the entire atmosphere.

5. Prophetic Worship Through History

During the **Welsh Revival (1904–1905)**, singing erupted spontaneously in coal mines, streets, and chapels. Bars shut down. Crime plummeted. Horses in coal pits had to be retrained because they were used to being cursed at, not sung over.

At **Azusa Street (1906)**, worship carried such prophetic weight that people walking blocks away could hear and feel the presence of God. Reports said the sound was like fire, like rushing waters, like heaven's own choir.

History proves: wherever prophetic sound rises, nations shift.

6. The Anatomy of Prophetic Sound

What makes worship prophetic? It carries at least three dimensions:

1. **It Reveals Heaven's Voice** — The Spirit gives utterance that goes beyond lyrics into living declaration.

2. **It Resists the Enemy** — Like Jehoshaphat's singers, it dismantles strategies of darkness.

3. **It Reframes Reality** — Prophetic sound lifts the church out of natural sight into kingdom perspective.

When a prophetic song is released, **earth bends to match heaven's decree.**

7. A Call to Modern Prophetic Worshippers

We must move beyond setlists that entertain or fill time. Prophetic worshippers must:

- Listen more than they perform.

- Sing scripture into atmospheres until strongholds collapse.

- Release new songs that become anthems for communities, cities, and nations.

- Carry songs into hospitals, prisons, and broken neighborhoods where no pulpit may ever stand.

The prophetic sound of worship is not confined to Sunday—it is a weapon in boardrooms, classrooms, and living rooms.

Prophetic Charge: Release the Sound!

Beloved, there is a sound in your spirit that hell cannot silence. When you release it, prisons will shake, nations will shift, and heaven will open. Don't just sing songs—**become the sound.**

The earth is groaning for the prophetic sound of worshippers who will not echo culture but will

declare the future of heaven into the present tense of earth.

Let it be said of our generation: *"They sang, and God moved. They worshipped, and nations bowed."*

CHAPTER 10:
WORSHIP THAT TOUCHES HEAVEN, CHANGES EARTH

_____

(Finale: worship not only encounters heaven but transforms communities, churches, families, and society)

WORSHIP THAT TOUCHES HEAVEN

Worship is not meant to stay locked in the sanctuary. Its ultimate purpose is transformation— hearts, homes, communities, and nations. If worship truly touches heaven, it will inevitably change the earth. Anything less is incomplete.

Heaven and Earth in Agreement

Jesus taught us to pray, *"Your kingdom come, your will be done, on earth as it is in heaven"* (Matthew 6:10 NIV). Worship is one of the primary ways heaven invades earth. Every time we declare God's glory, align our hearts, and enthrone Him in praise (Psalm 22:3), we are pulling heaven's reality into our earthly spaces.

In Isaiah 6, the prophet saw heavenly worship: seraphim crying, "Holy, holy, holy." That vision wrecked him. He was undone, transformed, and immediately commissioned to bring God's word to earth. Heaven's worship didn't just inspire Isaiah—it propelled him into mission.

Worship That Transforms Families

When a parent worships at home, the atmosphere shifts. Children sense the presence of God not through lectures but through environments saturated with worship. A house where worship is lifted becomes a sanctuary of peace. Marriages are healed as couples worship together, inviting God's glory to mend what words alone cannot.

Joshua declared, *"As for me and my household, we will serve the Lord"* (Joshua 24:15 NIV). Serving the Lord includes worship—it's the glue that keeps faith alive from one generation to the next.

Worship That Transforms Communities

In Acts 2, when the early believers worshiped and prayed, *"awe came upon everyone"* (v. 43). The result? Radical generosity, daily conversions, and societal transformation. Worship created a culture where no one was in need, where outsiders were drawn in, and where revival became visible in the streets.

Throughout church history, true revivals have always carried this mark: worship spilled outside church walls. Hymns echoed in coal mines during the Welsh Revival. Entire cities shut down bars and nightclubs during the Great Awakenings, because worship reshaped culture.

Worship That Confronts Darkness

In today's world, worship is not just devotional—it is confrontational. Every time believers lift their voices in praise, they declare that God reigns despite darkness. Worship establishes light in places of despair, hope in valleys of hopelessness, and peace in regions of chaos. It becomes a prophetic protest against the kingdom of darkness.

Psalm 149:6–9 paints a dramatic picture: *"May the praise of God be in their mouths and a double-edged sword in their hands..."* Praise is not passive. It binds rulers, confronts injustice, and executes the written judgment of God. Worship is warfare, and it transforms society when the church refuses to stay silent.

Worship as Revival's River

Ezekiel 47 describes a river flowing from the temple, bringing life wherever it goes. That is what worship does—it flows beyond the church doors into the streets, healing the sick, reviving the weary, and restoring the broken. True revival is not measured by how high people lift their hands inside church, but by how transformed a city becomes outside of it.

Closing Call

If revival is to last, worship must move from event to lifestyle, from stage to street, from Sunday to every day. The final picture of Scripture shows eternal worship: every tribe, nation, and tongue gathered around the throne (Revelation 7:9–10). But notice—the worship there is loud, public, transformative, and unending.

Worship that touches heaven will always change earth. It heals families, reforms communities, shifts nations, and glorifies Jesus until the kingdoms of this world become the kingdom of our Lord (Revelation 11:15).

PROPHETIC CHARGE:
A CALL TO WORSHIP-DRIVEN REVIVAL

WORSHIP THAT TOUCHES HEAVEN

Beloved, this is not just a book. This is a summons. Heaven is calling forth a generation who will worship beyond convenience, beyond routine, beyond self. A generation who will release the prophetic sound of heaven until nations tremble. A generation who will not settle for moments of His presence but will *host* Him daily.

Revival is not an event to be scheduled; it is a life to be lived. And revival is birthed, sustained, and multiplied through worship.

So I charge you:

- Sing with boldness.
- Pray with fire.
- Live with holiness.
- Release heaven's sound.
- Touch heaven. Change earth.

May your worship become the prophecy that awakens generations. May your song shift your city. May your life be the altar upon which heaven and earth continually meet.

This is the hour. This is the sound. This is revival.

www.ingramcontent.com/pod-product-compliance
Lightning Source LLC
Chambersburg PA
CBHW051710090426
42736CB00013B/2630